rainbow

It's Raining

Helena Ramsay and
Paul Humphrey

Illustrated by

Stuart Trotter

Evans

It hasn't rained for a long time. Look, these plants are drooping because they need water. Our pond is nearly empty too. If it doesn't rain soon the fish will die.

The grass looks burnt and brown.

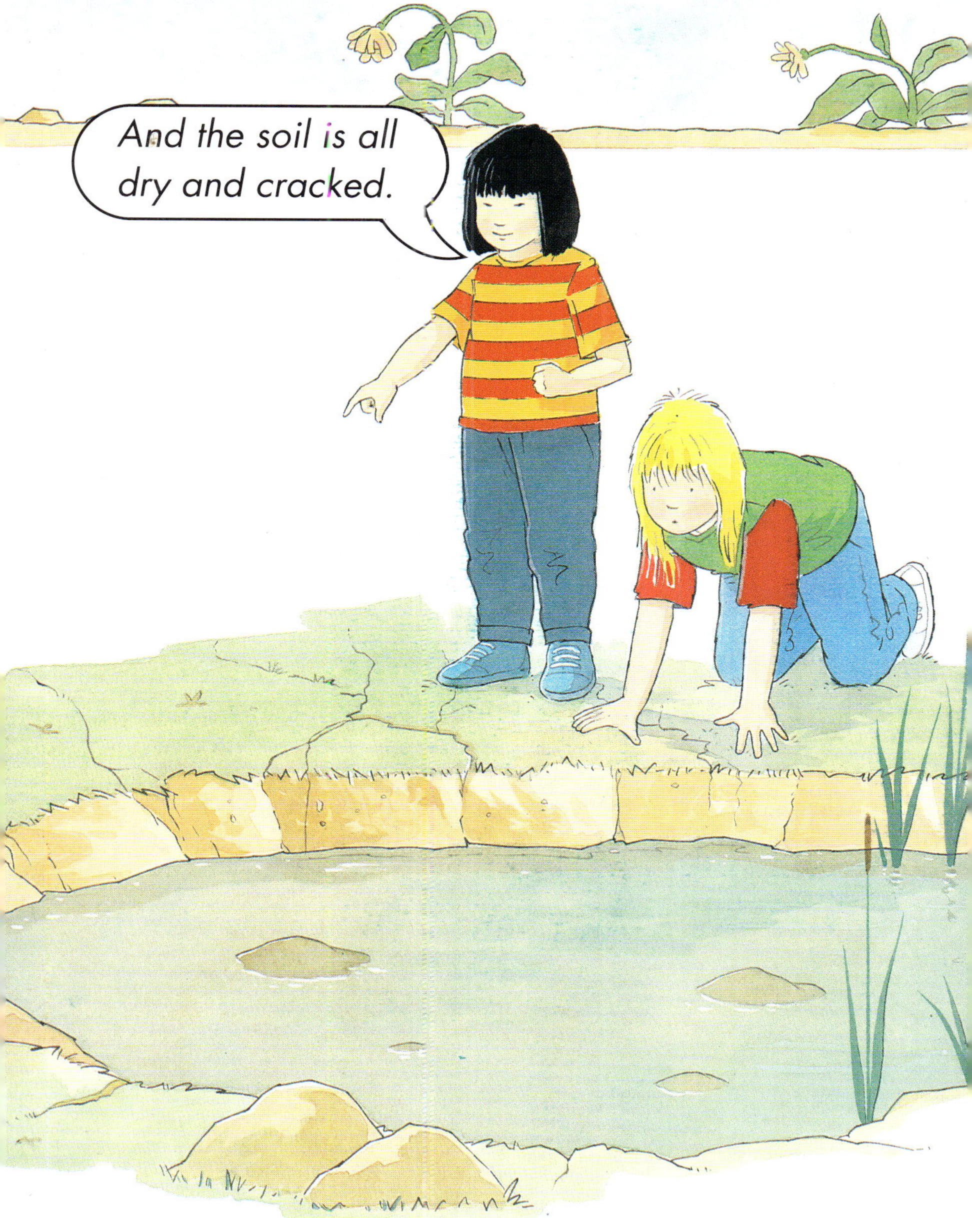
And the soil is all dry and cracked.

Look at those big black clouds. They are called cumulonimbus clouds and they usually bring rain.

They look black because they are so thick that the sun can't shine through them.

I think I can feel some raindrops already.

And that was a flash of lightning.

6

Let's run indoors.

7

Did you hear the thunder? You can tell how far away the storm is by counting the number of seconds between the flash of lightning and the thunder. Three seconds means the storm is one kilometre away.

Look, the rain has turned to hail.

You can see the hailstones bouncing on the path!

9

The storm has passed over and now it's only drizzling. Let's go out again and see what's happened.

Look, that bird has hopped into a puddle to have a bath.

It's splashing the water under its wings to get rid of the dust and bugs in its feathers.

11

> *Look at all the slugs and snails.*

Yes, they only come out after the rain or when it is nice and damp at night.

There are lots of worms in the flowerbed. Do they come out when it's wet, too?

Yes, they do.
If that bird sees them
it will gobble them up.

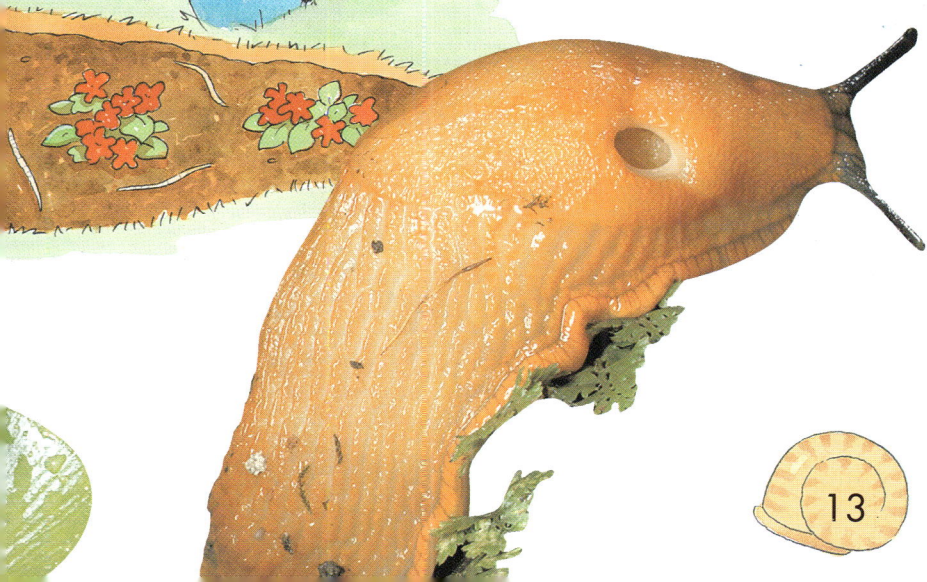

13

These plants needed the rain. They are not drooping any more. Now the sun has come out. Look at the raindrops on the leaves.

They look like diamonds sparkling in the sunshine.

15

Can you smell how fresh the air is? It always smells fresh after a rain storm.

And look, there is a beautiful rainbow.

Rainbows appear in the sky when the sun shines through the tiny drops of rain.

The wet road is steaming in the sun.

It's nearly dry already.

When water dries up like that it's called evaporation. The steam is called water vapour. It rises up into the sky and makes clouds again.

18

Climb into the basket of the balloon
and we'll go up into the clouds and
take a look.

19

Now we're rising up,
just like the water vapour.

*What happens to
the water vapour?*

It forms into rain clouds
and that means more rain.

Look down below at all the water in the rivers, lakes and seas. Some of that water turns into water vapour and makes rain clouds as well.

21

22

Water evaporates and turns into vapour
all the time, even when it is not sunny.

Now we are flying through the clouds. Can you feel how damp it is?

Yes, that's because the clouds are really water vapour.

How does the water vapour turn into rain?

Well, think of a kettle boiling. Steam comes out of the spout. When the steam touches a cool wall or window it turns back into water.

It is cold up here in the clouds.

When the water vapour rises into the sky it cools and turns back into millions of tiny drops of water.

The tiny drops join together to make bigger drops.

26

Then they fall
as rain.

27

Look at the water flowing
down that little river.
Where do you think that
water will go?

Down into the
big river.

Then down to the sea.

Then back into the
sky as clouds.

Then the clouds will
become rain again.
That is called the
water cycle.

Now we had better float
down to the ground, too,
and see if the rain has
filled our pond.

29

This picture shows the water cycle.
How many stages of the cycle can
you remember?